First Facts®

DATA MANIA

Analyzing Doggie Data

I'm Matt Maticus. I love mathematics! Collecting and analyzing information is an important part of math. Join me at the pet store, and I'll show you how!

by Marcie Aboff

Consultant:
Michele Koomen, PhD
Co-Chair and Assistant Professor of Education
Gustavus Adolphus College
St. Peter, Minnesota

CAPSTONE PRESS
a capstone imprint

First Facts is published by Capstone Press,
151 Good Counsel Drive, P.O. Box 669, Mankato, Minnesota 56002.
www.capstonepub.com

092010
005935LKS11

 Books published by Capstone Press are manufactured with paper
containing at least 10 percent post-consumer waste.

Library of Congress Cataloging-in-Publication Data
Aboff, Marcie.
  Analyzing doggie data / by Marcie Aboff.
    p. cm.—(First facts. Data mania)
  Summary: "Uses animals in a pet store to explore how collecting and analyzing data
can help readers organize and understand information"—Provided by publisher.
  Includes bibliographical references and index.
  ISBN 978-1-4296-4528-7 (library binding)
  ISBN 978-1-4296-6339-7 (paperback)
  1. Mathematical statistics—Juvenile literature. 2. Research—Methodology—Juvenile
literature. 3. Information management—Juvenile literature. I. Title. II. Series.

  QA273.16.A258 2011
  001.4'22—dc22   2010000548

Editorial Credits
Christopher L. Harbo, editor; Matt Bruning, designer and illustrator; Eric Manske,
    production specialist

Photo Credits
iStockphoto: Carlos Andres, cover (blackboard), Lise Gagne, 15 (goldfish), Stilyan
    Savov, background (throughout), Warwick Lister-Kaye, 21 (canaries),
Shutterstock: Alexey Avdeev, 11 (Persian cat), Alfredo Schaufelberger, 7 (puppy),
    alysta, 7 (lovebirds), Antonín Vodák, 7 (cat), Demark, 9 (blue parakeet), hagit
    berkovich, 9 (dog), Kati Molin, 11, 13 (grey cat), kristian sekulic, 9 (cat), Melinda
    Fawver, 5 (store), Mitch Aunger, 7 (goldfish), Sarah Holmlund, 9 (goldfish),
    Spauln, 11 (white cat)

Table of Contents

Digging into Data

A pet store is a great place to gather **data**. Data is a collection of facts or information that tells a story about something. Data can tell us the types of food a hamster eats. It can also tell us which toys a dog plays with every day.

data—information or facts

Let's find out how much data we can gather at the pet store!

Collect and Compare

Wow, this store is packed with data! I see dogs, cats, birds, and fish. Let's find out how many animals live here. Counting is a great way to collect data. I'll count all of the animals. Then I can **record** the data I collect in my notepad.

record—to write down information so that it can be kept

After you collect data, you can **compare** what you've found. This bar graph shows us that the store has more fish than dogs. Use the bar graph to compare the number of cats and birds. Uh-oh! There are more cats. The birds better watch out!

compare—to judge one thing against another

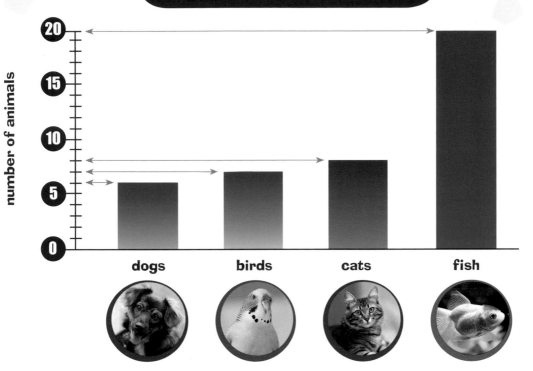

Pet Store Animals

number of animals

20
15
10
5
0

dogs   birds   cats   fish

Comparing within Groups

You can also compare animals within their own groups.
For example, you can compare all the cats' fur color. Some cats
have black fur, some have white fur, and some are mixed. You
can also compare the dogs' sizes or the different kinds of birds.

Seeing Is Believing

Observation is another way to collect data. Flo, Jo, and Mo love taking catnaps. I wanted to know which cat sleeps the most. I used a watch to time each cat sleeping. By the end of the day, Flo had slept three hours. Jo had slept two hours. Mo had slept six hours! Whoa, Mo's a big snoozer!

observation—the careful watching of someone or something

Catnaps

Flo → **3 hours**

Jo → **2 hours**

Mo → **6 hours**

After you **analyze** data, you might need more information. I want to know how much Mo sleeps during the week. I need to collect more data.

This line graph shows how much Mo slept. Each dot shows the number of hours he slept each day. What day did Mo nap the longest? What day did he sleep the least? Which two days did Mo snooze the same amount of time?

analyze—to examine something carefully in order to understand it

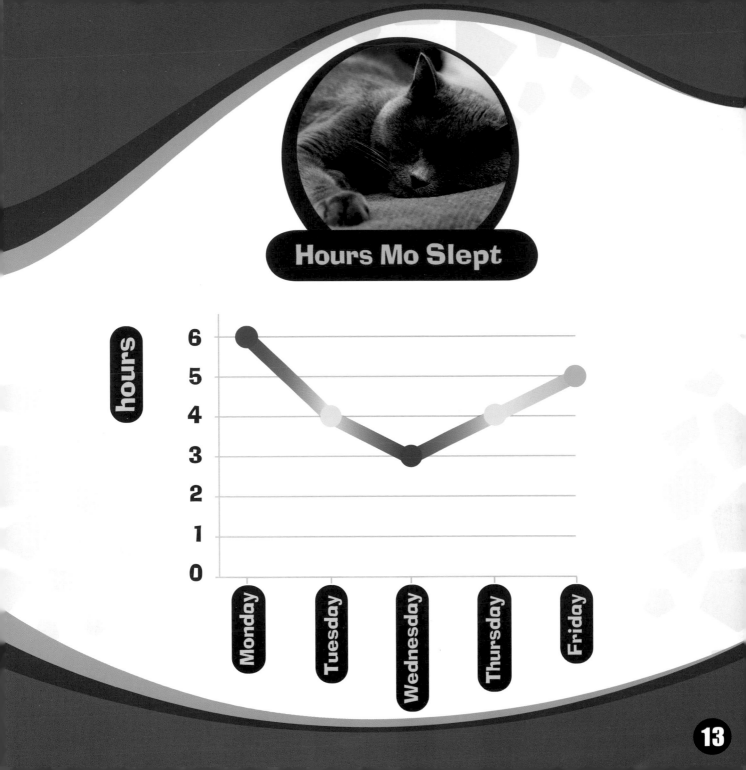

Hours Mo Slept

Asking Questions

Asking questions also helps you collect data. When I visited the fish, they were gobbling three types of fish food. I wondered which food they liked best, so I asked them.

I collected my data and made a pictograph to show what I found. What food do the fish like best? More fish like flakes than worms or pellets.

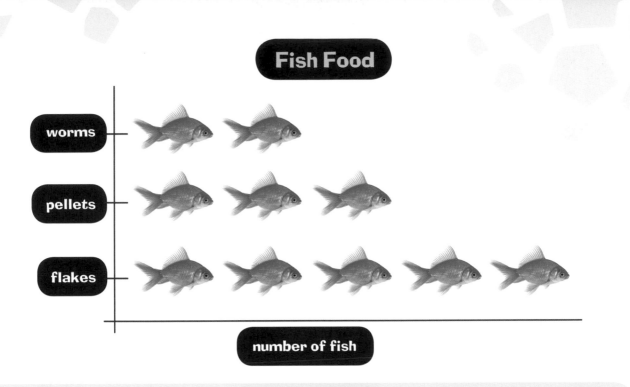

Fish Food

worms

pellets

flakes

number of fish

Pie Graphs

You can also use a pie graph to show the answers you found. A pie graph is shaped like a circle. The graph stands for a whole group of something. The graph is divided into sections based on the food. Count the number of sections to see which food the fish liked best.

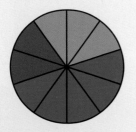

fish that like worms

fish that like pellets

fish that like flakes

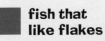

Finding an Average

A great way to analyze data is to find an **average**. The hamster loves his spinning wheel. I wanted to know the average number of times he uses it each day.

I watched him for five days. I recorded the number of times he used the wheel each day. I added the number of times together. Then I divided the total number of times by five days. He used the wheel an average of six times a day.

average—a single number that describes a larger collection of numbers

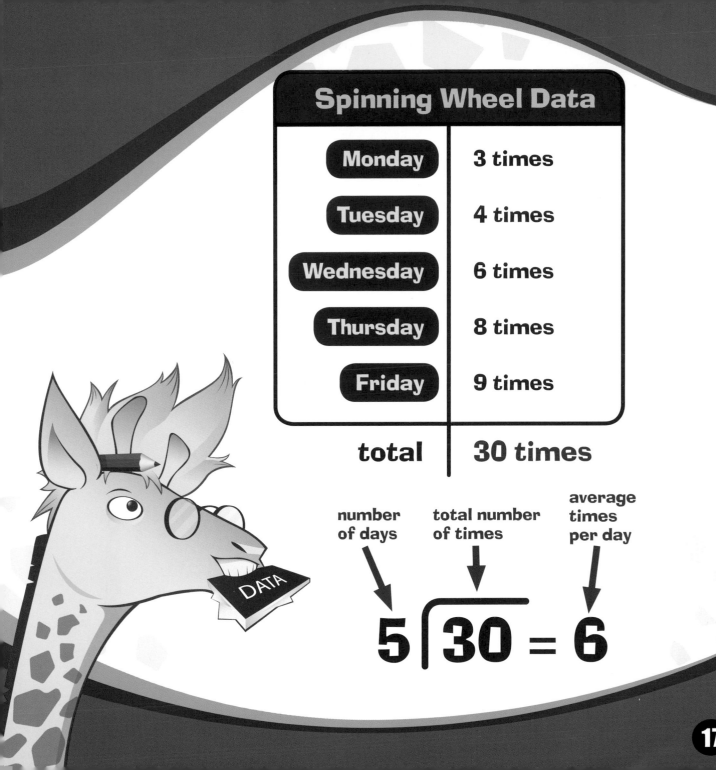

Spinning Wheel Data

Monday	3 times
Tuesday	4 times
Wednesday	6 times
Thursday	8 times
Friday	9 times
total	30 times

number of days

total number of times

average times per day

$$5\overline{)30} = 6$$

Check Out the Range

When you analyze data, you can also see the **range** of the data. For example, the pet store opens at 10:00 in the morning. It closes at 6:00 at night. I wanted to see what time of day the store is most crowded. I counted the number of customers in the pet store each hour. I used the data to make a chart. Can you tell when the store was most crowded?

range—the difference between the least and greatest in a set of data

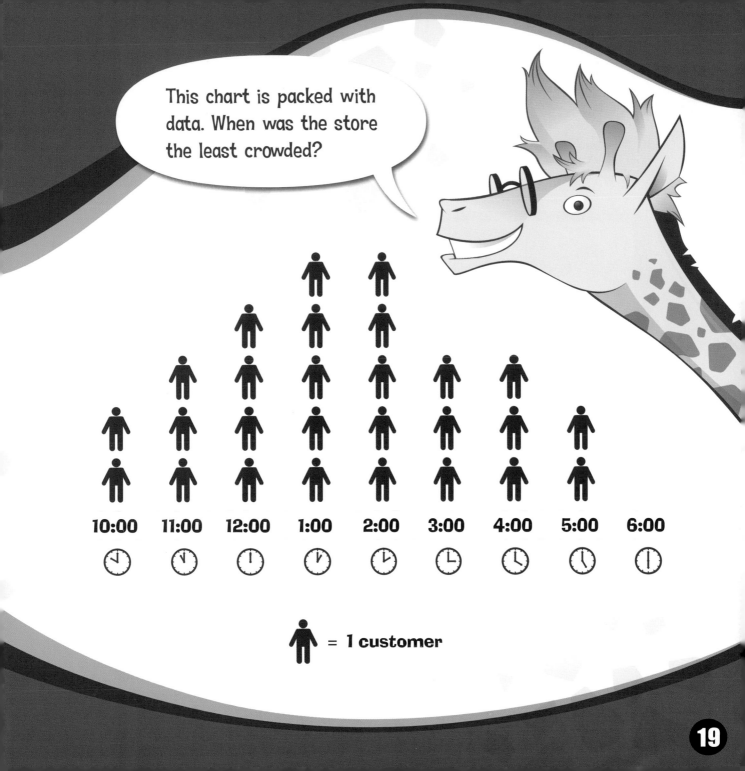

Solving Problems

Collecting and analyzing data can solve even the noisiest problems. The birds love singing. But the other animals are arguing about the songs they want to hear. This is a perfect time to collect more data. I'll ask each animal which song they like best. Then the birds will know which songs to sing. What will data say about your world? Start collecting and find out!

Glossary

analyze (AN-uh-lize)—to examine something carefully in order to understand it

average (A-vuh-rij)—a single number that describes a larger collection of numbers

compare (kuhm-PAYR)—to judge one thing against another and note the similarities and differences

data (DAY-tuh)—information or facts

divide (duh-VIDE)—to figure out how many times one number will go into another number

observation (ob-zur-VAY-shuhn)—the careful watching of someone or something

range (RAYNJ)—the difference between the least and greatest in a set of data

record (ri-KORD)—to write down information so that it can be kept

Read More

Besel, Jennifer M. *Lions and Tigers and Graphs! Oh My!* Data Mania. Mankato, Minn.: Capstone Press, 2011.

Harris, Nancy. *Mashed Potatoes: Collecting and Reporting Data.* Vero Beach, Fla: Rourke Publishing, 2008.

Internet Sites

FactHound offers a safe, fun way to find Internet sites related to this book. All of the sites on FactHound have been researched by our staff.

Here's all you do:

Visit *www.facthound.com*

FactHound will fetch the best sites for you!

Index